Think and Link

An advanced course in reading and writing skills

Janelle Cooper

Edward Arnold

© Janelle Cooper 1979

First published 1979
by Edward Arnold (Publishers) Ltd
41 Bedford Square, London WC1B 3DQ

British Library Cataloguing in Publication Data
Cooper, Janelle
  Think and link.
  1. English language – Text-books for foreigners
  2. English language – Composition and exercises
  I. Title
  808'.042'076   PE1128

  ISBN 0–7131–0315–9

Phototypeset in 11/12 pt. V.I.P. Palatino by
Western Printing Services Ltd, Bristol
and printed in Great Britain by
Unwin Brothers Ltd,
The Gresham Press, London and Old Woking

CONTENTS

Student's Notes

Purpose

This book is to help you write more organised English and to help you select and order facts from reading passages.

Background

As you know, writing in another language is not just translating words from one language to the other. Each language has its own way of organising ideas – what is acceptable in English may not be acceptable in your language, and vice versa. So, in order to understand fully and to write well, you need to be able to recognise and use the acceptable ways of organising ideas in English.

Description

In the book you are shown the four main connections between ideas in English: sequencing, classification, comparison and contrast, cause and effect. In each unit you are given the words and expressions we most commonly use to show these links.

Then, you have exercises, both short and long, to practise selecting and using these. In the work on reading, you are asked to extract the main facts from a passage, and to put them into a different form. Since the book is concerned with writing that conveys information, you will also learn about such devices as charts, tables, graphs. These ways of showing information are also useful as a method of note taking, to help you understand and remember ideas and the connections between them.

Topics

As you do the exercises you will learn about a variety of subjects, e.g. (for example) coffee growing, inflation, binoculars. You can apply the techniques you learn with these to other topics you are interested in.

If you are using this book without a teacher, read through the Teacher's Notes for suggestions for further work.

Teacher's Notes

Purpose

The aim of this book is to help advanced overseas students to read and write English through the presentation and practice of the ways in which ideas and information are organised in English. Many students can write grammatically correct sentences but fail to progress in English because they are unable to organise their ideas in a manner acceptable to an English reader. Similarly, though they understand individual sentences, students fail to comprehend extended pieces of writing because they are unable to see the organisation of the ideas. This book will help such students. In addition, it will be valuable to students

a. who are studying or going to study other subjects through the medium of English in their own countries or in an English-speaking country.
b. who are going to take examinations such as the Cambridge Certificate of Proficiency and the Joint Matriculation Board Test in English (Overseas).
c. who need to use written English in their jobs.

It will also develop the skills necessary for note taking and summary writing.

Organisation and Grading

The book is divided into the four main ways of organising ideas and information in English:

1. Sequencing
2. Classification
3. Comparison and Contrast
4. Cause and Effect

These are in order of difficulty, from the easier to the more difficult. Each section is dependent, to a certain extent, on the former one(s). The material within each unit is also graded from easy to difficult. Thus, it is possible to work through the whole book in order, or to do, for example, the first half of each unit for the first four units, followed by the second half.

Subject Matter

There is a wide range of subject matter, and many of the topics in the reading and writing exercises will be unfamiliar to the students. This is deliberate, so that the students are actively learning through English; the organisational skills acquired are readily transferable to other topics.

Vocabulary

Much of the vocabulary will also be strange to the students. This is to encourage the students to use the subject matter, their general knowledge and the context to make 'intelligent guesses' as to the meaning of words. It is also useful in training them to ignore, temporarily, those unfamiliar words whose meaning is not essential to the understanding of the passage.

Student Research

When students are particularly interested in or stimulated by a topic, they should, where possible, be encouraged to undertake further work on the subject through library research, projects and/or visits to appropriate places.

Graphic Presentation

Since much information today is presented in a graphic way, and since the use of graphics is a helpful and common way of ordering and remembering information, much of the material in this book is presented graphically. The devices employed include diagrams, maps, tables, bar charts and curve graphs. The student will practise extracting information from, and ordering ideas through, the use of such types of graphics.

Types of Exercise
There are many different types of exercise in this book:

ordering and reordering information
filling in tables, charts, graphs
marking routes on a map
labelling diagrams
drawing simple diagrams

The writing exercises include paragraph construction based on given information and on the student's own ideas, and essay writing from given information and the student's own ideas.

Method
In a classroom, this book can be used for individual work, or for group work followed by individual work. In the latter method, students work in pairs or small groups to discuss the exercises and work through them orally before beginning to write. This is recommended, where possible, to encourage the stimulation and exchange of ideas. When an exercise has been completed, students should compare answers and discuss differences.

At the beginning of most units and sections, a list and examples of common connectives are given. Students should suggest appropriate sentences using these. The student's attention has not been explicitly drawn to the grammatical force of the various connectives, e.g. adverb/conjunction. However, the use of the connectives is made clear in the examples.

After the students have completed the reading exercises, the teacher may like to point out the examples of word-families in the text and to use these for word-building practice.

The following section shows what general areas of grammar are made use of, but not *taught*, in each unit. Suggestions for extension work and comments on specific exercises are also given.

Sequencing
This unit deals with three kinds of sequencing:

instructions – using imperatives
processes – using the simple present tense and passives
writing about past events – using the past tenses and participial forms

Recipes
Students can write their own recipes, then jumble the order of instructions for other members of the group/class to put into the correct order.

Bicycle Puncture. Pottery Throwing
Students write instructions for other simple tasks they know about, e.g. changing a car wheel.

Letter Sorting
This could be the basis for a project by the students, e.g. how letter-sorting differs in their country; what happens to the letters after they have been delivered to the railway station.

Wine Making. Coffee Growing
These also lend themselves to project work. Students select a manufactured article and/or agricultural product of their country and describe the processes involved in an essay, with a diagram. Library research and visits should be encouraged for this.

Louis Pasteur
Students discuss and select the most important events in his life, and then write a 3–4 sentence summary, suitable for an encyclopedia entry.

Christopher Wren
Students choose an important/interesting person from the history of their country, summarise the information in list form, and then write an essay on him/her – possibly without mentioning any names, so the other students must identify the subject.

Classification

This unit uses countables/uncountables and articles.

Categories 1
Students compare their list of examples and classifications with those of others in the group/class, and discuss differences. They could also offer suggestions for other groups to be exemplified and classified.

House Types
Students describe houses in their country and classify them according to the categories of the passage. They should devise new categories if needed. Pictures of houses could also be used for the same purpose.

Definitions
There is no explicit work on word building in the book, but this exercise will help students see how words are built in English. The functions and meanings of affixes could usefully be brought into this section.

Dam Types
Students write descriptions of those dams which have been labelled 'X', i.e. not described in the passage.

Television
Other paragraphs, either from earlier in the book or outside, could also be jumbled. Students should be encouraged to use outside knowledge, as well as language clues, to help them reorder the sentences.

Comparison and Contrast

Comparatives of countables and uncountables occur in this section.

Colour TV Sets. Binoculars Through their own research in shops etc. students can build up similar tables, from which to write recommendations.

Tables and Charts
Students draw their own bar charts and curve graphs showing information about their own country from government reports etc. They can also devise exercises similar to those in this section, i.e. deleting figures or parts of their graphs, and from their written reports on the information, other students in the group/class complete the graph.

Cause and Effect

Forms of modality are used here.

Plants
This work can be extended to human ailments. A student describes his/her symptoms, e.g. headache, high temperature, and the other students suggest appropriate diagnoses. Possible explanations can also be practised in other situations, such as a detective investigating a crime or an insurance agent investigating a car accident. Such questions as, 'How do you think it happened? Why?' may be asked.

How it Works
It is helpful if students can use real objects in this exercise, e.g. they bring in a ball-point pen, dismantle it and put it together again. Then they show and explain to other students how it works. When they don't know the exact word for part of the object, they should use alternative expressions, such as 'a sort of . . .', 'a type of . . .', 'it's like . . .' or analogies.

Reference

There are many examples of this in the book, e.g. in Bicycle tyres and Letter sorting. Students can look back at the earlier passages and find examples of such words and what they refer to.

Inflation. Bird Droppings

Students prepare summaries in the form of diagrams etc. from their outside knowledge and reading, to use as the basis for short talks about the subject to other students in their group/class.

Acknowledgments

The Publisher wishes to thank the following for permission to reproduce copyright material:

The Joint Matriculation Board, Manchester for the use of questions from the Test in English (Overseas) Papers: *June 1974*, Questions 1 (Coffee Growing), 3A (Chinampa Farming), 3B (Bus Routes) and 3C (Wine-making); *March 1976*, 1 (Education Systems), 4B (House Types); *June 1976*, 1 (Skiing), 2 (Pottery Throwing), 4A (Energy), 4B (Water Shortage); *March 1977*, 1 (Port of Wye) and *June 1977*, 4A (Dam Types and Big Ben); Penguin Books, in association with Her Majesty's Stationery Office, for Charts 15 (University full-time students), 21 (Leisure activities: cinema and television), 28 (Total inland energy consumption: United Kingdom) from *Facts in Focus*, fourth edition 1978, pp. 114, 137, 167 Crown copyright 1972, 1974, 1975, 1978 ©; 'Which?' magazine for extracts from 1976 Binoculars and TV Reports, by permission of the Consumers' Association; 'Bird droppings in Peru' is taken from the University of Cambridge Local Examination Syndicate's Certificate of Proficiency in English paper, Part I, 13 June 1973; the letter sorting diagram from the Mount Pleasant (London) Postal Guide PL/266 5/68; and Penguin Books for an extract from Claudia Roden's *A Book of Middle Eastern Food*.

Making an omelette

1.

2. Beat lightly

3. Salt   Pepper

4.

5. Butter hot, not brown

6.

7. Mixture sets

8.

x

Sequencing

1 Recipes

When we give instructions we use the imperative: do this or don't do that, and we try to put the instructions for doing a job in the order or sequence in which they have to be done.

a Now read the instructions for cooking rice.

How to cook plain rice
Ingredients:

  2 teacups long-grain rice
  2 teacups water
  salt

Method:

1. Boil two cups of salted water in a saucepan.
2. Put in two cups of rice.
3. Bring to the boil again.
4. Boil rice quickly for 2 minutes.
5. Cover the pan with a tight-fitting lid.
6. Simmer the rice gently for about 20 minutes, until the water has been absorbed and the rice is cooked.

b Now write out the instructions for making an omelette. Use the drawings opposite to help you put them into the correct sequence.

c Below are some instructions for making lentil and vegetable stew, but they are in the wrong order. Put the letters next to each instruction into the right sequence. The first one has been done for you.

Lentil and vegetable stew
Ingredients:

  $\frac{1}{4}$ kilo lentils, soaked overnight if necessary.
  2 medium potatoes, peeled and coarsely cubed.
  $\frac{1}{4}$ kilo courgettes, sliced and cubed.
  $\frac{1}{4}$ kilo leeks, trimmed and sliced.
  1 stalk celery, sliced.
  salt and pepper.
  1 onion, finely chopped.
  oil.
  2 cloves garlic, crushed.
  2 tablespoons finely chopped parsley.
  juice of two lemons.

Method:

A. Add the potatoes, courgettes, leeks and celery.
B. Fry the onion in oil until soft and golden.
C. Season to taste with salt and pepper, and continue cooking for 15 to 20 minutes longer.
D. Drain and add to the lentils and vegetables, together with parsley and lemon juice.
E. Drain soaked lentils and simmer in a large saucepan in $\frac{1}{2}$ litre water for about $1\frac{1}{4}$ hours, or until nearly soft.
F. Add garlic and fry for a minute or two longer until coloured.
G. Simmer for a few minutes longer, adjust seasoning and serve hot or cold.

  1. E.   2.   3.   4.   5.   6.   7.

1

2 Bus routes

Here we have a description of two bus routes. Mark the two bus routes on the following map. Use a broken line (– – – – –) for the special bus and an unbroken line (———) for the 67 bus. Remember all these are two-way streets, with traffic going in each direction. You do not need to understand all the words in order to fill in the map.

You can see a certain amount of the city by travelling on the 67 bus which goes from the bus station to the museum three times a day. However it is best for the visitor to take a tour of the city on the special bus which is provided by the corporation at a nominal charge especially for the purpose.

Both buses come out of the bus station and turn left. The first place of interest the visitor passes if he goes on the 67 bus is the public gardens, which the bus reaches by taking the first turn left and going to the end of the road. However the special bus continues to the end of the road after leaving the bus station, turns left and drives slowly past the castle. If anyone is specially interested he can make a special request for the bus to stop at the castle. However such a stop must be arranged in advance so that a guide will be available to conduct the passengers around the castle. After this the special bus takes the first corner to the right and stops at the docks. On the way it passes the station which has an interesting Victorian façade.

The sightseeing bus waits at the docks for about 10 minutes to enable the passengers to get out and walk around. It then goes straight up the road from the docks and takes the fourth corner on the right. Here the routes of the two buses converge for the first time.

Both buses turn right and begin to drive round the outside of the gardens. Then the routes diverge again. The sightseeing bus takes the first road to the left while the other bus continues round the gardens and drives straight to the sea front. The special bus stops at Browns Hill for several minutes to let the passengers look at the view of the city spread out below them. It then goes directly to the sea front. Both buses eventually travel along the sea front, take the third corner to the left and continue along the street until they come to the museum.

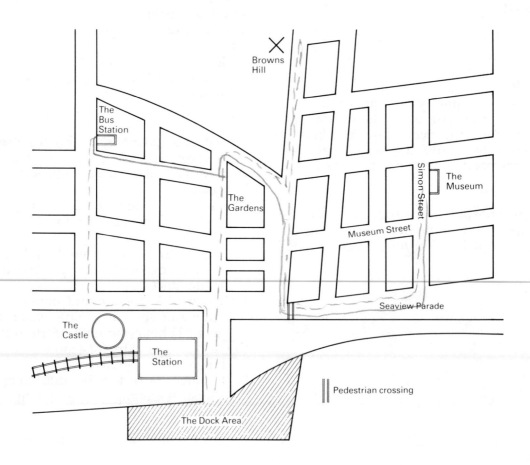

2

3 Mending a puncture

Here is some informal advice on how to begin mending a flat bicycle tyre. Below the passage is the same advice, this time written out in the form of instructions.

a Using the information in the passage and the diagram to help you, complete the instructions.

How to mend a flat bicycle tyre

Flat tyres are often caused by punctures which leak air with varying degrees of speed. Punctures which are not huge holes can be repaired. You'll need a tube patch kit containing patches, glue, an abrasive surface e.g. sandpaper, tyre irons and chalk.

You should begin by deflating the tyre. But first of all, it'd be a good idea to check if the flat tyre is just due to a faulty valve. You can do this by placing a drop of spit or water on the end of the valve stem. A leaky valve will bubble or spit back. In this case, just tighten the valve. However, if there is no fault in the valve, you should begin, as mentioned before, by deflating the tyre. Then you should work the tyre back and forth with your hands to get the edge of the tyre free of the rim. If this doesn't work, use the tyre irons as levers to free the tyre. When the edge is off the rim, you should push the valve stem up into the tyre, and remove the tube. At this stage you should inflate the tube and rotate it past your ear. If you can find the puncture through the hiss of escaping air, it's a good idea to mark the spot with chalk. If you can't, then you should place all of the tube in water, look for escaping air bubbles, and then mark the spot.

1. Place a drop of spit or water on the end of the tyre valve stem.
2. If there are bubbles, tighten the valve.
   If not,
3. Deflate the tyre
4. Either
   (a) Work the tyre back and forth with your hands to get the edge of the tyre free of the rim
   or
   (b) Use the tyre irons as levers to free the tyre.
5. Push the valve stem up into the tyre.

b Now write the instructions for putting on the patch and replacing the tube.

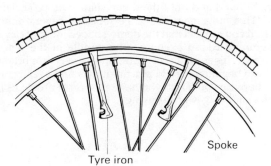

Tyre iron   Spoke

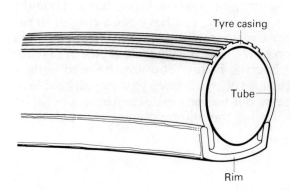

Tyre casing

Tube

Rim

3

4 Pottery throwing

When we talk, usually our words and expressions are simpler than when we write, and often, our ideas are not as well organised as they are when we write. Below is a talk on throwing pottery. You will be asked to reorganise it.

Throwing pottery

One way of making pottery is to use a potter's wheel. There are many types of wheel but the basic pattern is illustrated in the following diagram.

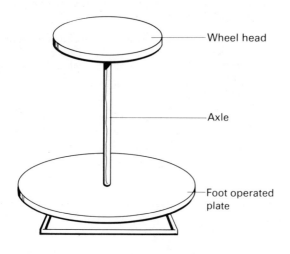

The process of making a pot on such a wheel is called throwing. There are three stages in throwing, the first of which is called centring. Imagine your workshop has just bought a new wheel. You have been elected to represent your colleagues at a series of lectures on how to use the wheel and part of Lecture 1 is given below. You now have to write a clear set of instructions so they will be able to carry out the process of centring.

Using the information given below in Lecture 1, write a clear set of instructions suitable for pinning on the wall by the wheel. Try to picture each step in your mind as you read.

Lecture 1
'Well, one of the most important things in centring is the way you move – you have to keep your elbows pressed firmly against your body, otherwise you lose control of what you are doing. Now, after you've prepared the clay so that it's neither too moist nor too stiff, and so that it's well-mixed throughout, you roll it into a round ball and put it on the wheel head ready for centring. (Make sure that you have dipped your hands in water before you start.) When you are beginning you shouldn't have a ball that's too big. It should fit comfortably between your two hands. You turn the wheel with your foot and as it begins turning round you put your hands round the lump so that the fingers of your right hand overlap your left hand. Then you press inwards so that the clay rises into a cone shape – when you're doing it remember to keep your palms vertical or you'll get into difficulties. Then you've got to flatten the cone into a sort of dome. You do it by pressing down with your palms and thumbs. The lower area of your palms should keep the clay from flattening right out so that you keep a dome shape. Another way of flattening the cone is to have your hands interlocked. Then you press down with your right hand and hold the dome shape with your left.

'This movement has to be repeated several times until you can feel that the dome-shaped lump of clay is spinning round evenly in the middle of the wheel head. This is called centring and is very important, and a beginner should practise it over and over again, otherwise you'll find you have all sorts of problems in the later stages of throwing. . . .'

4

5 Processes: connectives and useful expressions

a To help our readers we use conjunctions or links in order to show them how our ideas are connected. The following are some of the links we can use to show the sequence in which things happen.

Firstly,	The first step is
First of all,	The first stage is
To begin with,	begins with
	commences with
Beforehand,	Before this,
Previously,	Prior to this,
Earlier,	
At the same time,	During
Simultaneously,	
Secondly,	After this,
Next,	The next step is
Then,	In the next stage,
Subsequently,	In the following stage,
Later,	
Eventually,	finishes with
Finally,	concludes with
In the last stage,	The last step is

b The following are useful expressions when describing processes.

step – one action in a series of actions.
stage – a point or period of time in a series of actions.
process – a series of steps; a way in which something happens or is done.
procedure – the order of doing things.

e.g. In the wine-making process, the procedure is as follows. The first step is to take the grapes from the vines to the winery. Speed is essential at this stage.

takes place	by means of
is carried out	using
occurs	with the help of
	through

One method of . . . . is to
One of the ways of . . . . is to

5

6 Letter sorting

a   Here is a description of the process of sorting letters. Notice that the passive form of the verb is used a lot. This is because in this type of writing, we are usually more interested in the process than in the people doing the work. Underline all the link words.

First of all, letters and packets are collected in bags from pillar boxes, post offices and firms, in post office vans. They are then taken to the sorting office, where the bags are emptied and the letters separated from the packets. Following this step, the letters are put through machines so that the stamps can be cancelled. In this process the date and place of sorting are put over the stamps on each envelope. In the next stage, the sorting of the letters takes place, according to the county they are addressed to. This is done by placing them in the appropriate pigeon hole. Subsequently, the letters are taken from the pigeon holes and placed in baskets, which are then put onto a conveyor belt. While on this conveyor belt, the baskets are directed to the appropriate secondary sorting section by means of coding pegs. At the secondary sorting frames, the letters are put into towns in the county. Later, the letters are tied in bundles and a label is put on showing the towns they are addressed to. Finally, the letter bundles are placed in bags, which have the Post Office seal, Post Office Railway number and Destination Code number on them, and then these are sent to the railway station.

b   Now using the information in the passage and the diagram, fill in the chart below. Not every space needs to be filled in. The first one has been done for you.

Step	Place	Action
1	Pillar boxes	Letters collected (The letters are collected)
2		
3		
4		
5		
6		
7		
8		

We could also organise the actions or process into main and less important stages: main and sub-stages, e.g. main stages:
   Collection
   Sorting
   Distribution

The sub-stages of sorting would be:
   Separation of letters and packets
   Stamp cancelling
   Primary sorting into counties
   Secondary sorting into towns

6

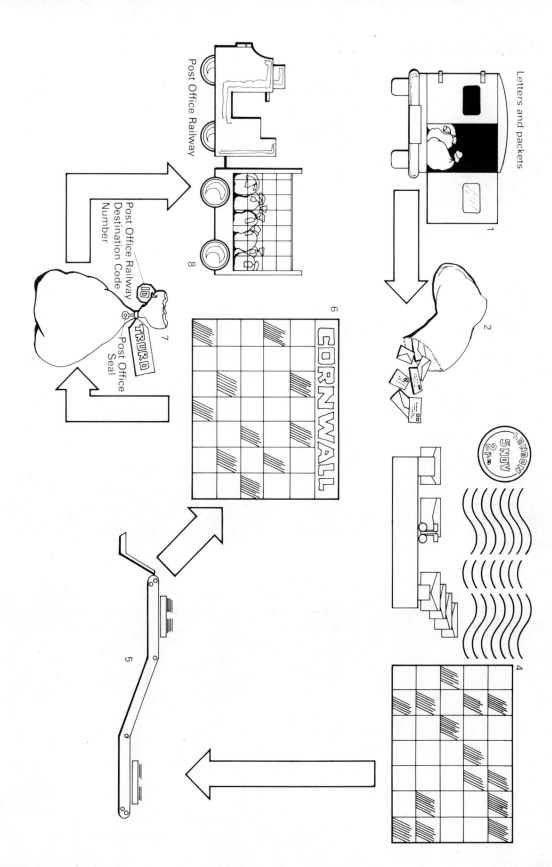

Letters and packets

Post Office Railway

Post Office Railway
Destination Code
Number

Post Office
Seal

TRURO

CORNWALL

LONDON
5 NOV
2 p.m.

7

7 Wine making

The following passage is about wine making. Think about this subject before you begin to read. What do you know about wine making? What do grapes look like? How is grape-juice different from wine? Then, as you read, try to picture each step of the process in your mind. When you meet an unfamiliar word, use the subject matter and the surrounding words and expressions, i.e. the context, to help you make an intelligent guess at the meaning.

Wine making is a very complicated process. However it can be said that in the twentieth century wine making has become a reasonably well understood art.

Let's look at the steps involved in the process of turning grapes into a drinkable wine, taking as our example the typical procedure in a modern Californian winery.

For all types of wine the grapes are taken from vine to winery as quickly and carefully as possible to minimise their loss of water and sugar after picking and to prevent spoilage.

At the winery they are immediately put into a crusher which crushes the skins, freeing pulp and juice without breaking the seeds, and which removes the stems and ejects them. After the removal of the stems and the crushing, in the case of white wine, the juice is pressed out at this point and sent alone to the fermenting vat. However in the case of red wine, after the removal of the stems the entire contents of the crusher go into the fermentation process. The red wine will take its colour and flavour from substances in skin and seeds.

In the fermentation vat the first step is the addition of sulphur dioxide to prevent the growth of natural yeasts which will have a bad effect on the quality of the wine. These are replaced by the addition of pure cultures of yeast to cause fermentation. The duration of fermentation in a modern winery varies from a few

days to a few weeks depending on the temperature, type of yeast used, sugar content of grapes and type of wine to be produced. A period longer than a few weeks makes the wine very bitter.

When part of the sugar content has been converted to alcohol and adequate colour has been extracted from the pulp the liquid is pressed out of the pulp by the wine press which ejects the skins and seeds.

The juice then proceeds from the fermentation stage to the stages of clearing and ageing. For clarification the fermented juice goes to the first of the settling vats where suspended yeast cells and small particles of pulp and stem rapidly settle out of the liquid and sink to the bottom of the vat. The clearing wine is skimmed several times and passed into the second settling vat where 'fining' substances are added to assist the clearing process. These are substances such as bentonite clay, gelatine, egg white or isinglass.

Ageing of the now clear juice begins in a wooden cask. The amount of oxidation by means of oxygen absorbed through pores in the wood of the cask is important here. It takes two years for a good red wine and two months to a year for a white wine.

After bottling, ageing continues. It is a fallacy to believe however that the longer wine stays in the bottle the better it is. As a general rule white wine has reached its peak after 2 to 5 years. For good red wine 5 to 10 years in a bottle is long enough.

8

Now using information from the passage, complete the following table about the making of *RED* wine:

i Label all the arrows in the diagram (columns I to VII). A broken arrow $--\rightarrow$ indicates removal. Some arrows, both broken and unbroken, will have more than one word. Use all the following words:

seeds   stems   yeast   juice ageing wine   pulp   skins clearing juice   skins   seeds sulphur dioxide   juice   gelatine cleared juice   egg whites.

ii Under the diagram, write the place where each step in the process takes place and write the name of the step (columns I–VII). Use the following words:

settling vat   cask   ageing (oxidation) clearing   crusher   de-stemming ageing   fermentation vat   de-skinning   settling vat   fermentation   clearing   bottle   wine press separation of liquid.

iii Write the time taken for the parts of the process given in columns II, VI and VII.

RED WINE

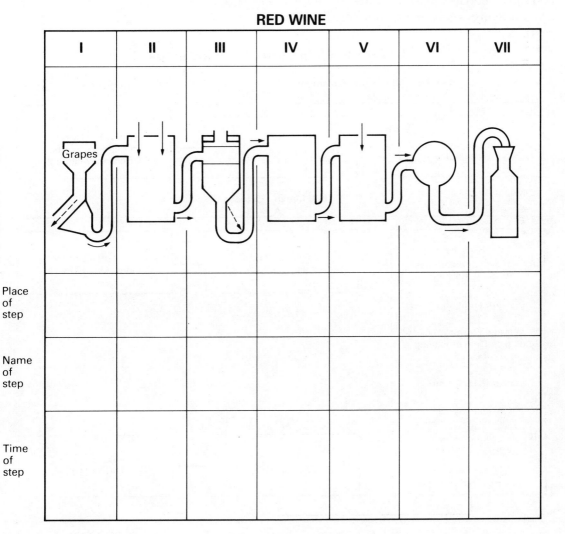

	I	II	III	IV	V	VI	VII
Place of step							
Name of step							
Time of step							

9

8 Purpose: connectives

When describing a process we generally include why the process was carried out. The following connectives are often used:

to; not to; in order to; in order not to; so as to; so as not to; so that; with the purpose of.

e.g. The grapes are taken from vine to winery as quickly and carefully as possible
to minimise their loss of water.

Or we could say   *in order to* minimise
so as to minimise
with the purpose of minimising
so that their loss of water is minimised

9 Coffee growing

Here is a diagram which gives you information about coffee growing in Brazil. Imagine you have been asked to write about coffee in a small reference book on the world's commercial crops. Remember to use the passive form of verbs, link words and connectives of purpose.

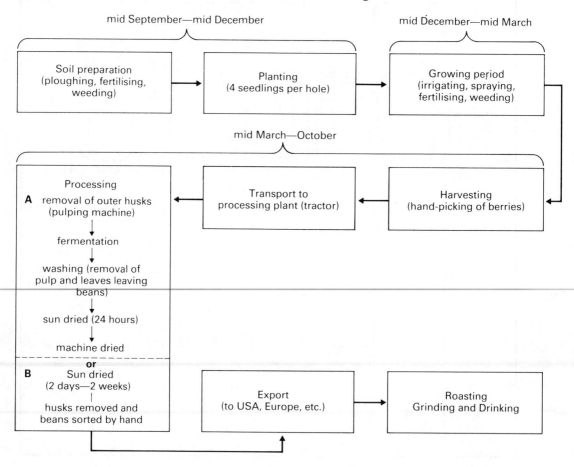

A Year's Work in Coffee Growing in Brazil

10 Past Events: connectives

When we are writing about past events, the order in which things happened is often very important. To make the order clear to our readers, we mention dates and time, and we also use various links and connectives.

One Before The Other

1. He finished his studies at the university.   2. He went to London.

When
As soon as he *had* finished his studies at the university, he went to London.
After

Before he went to London, he *had* finished his studies at the university.

On finish*ing* his studies, he went to London.

After finish*ing* his studies,   he went to London.
Having finish*ed* his studies,

Before go*ing* to London, he *had* finished his studies.

1. He was accepted by the university.   2. He started reading for his course.

On being accept*ed* by the university,   he started reading for his course.
Having been accept*ed* by the university,

At The Same Time

He studied at university. He made an important discovery.

While he was studying at university, he made an important discovery.

When study*ing* at university, he made an important discovery.
While

During his *studies* at university, he made an important discovery.

11 Louis Pasteur

Below is a list of dates and a summary of the main events in the life of this famous nineteenth-century French scientist. Then there is a passage based on the list. Read the passage and underline the time connections – links and verbs – used.

	People's belief in spontaneous generation
	L.P.'s father in army
1822	Birth. Father a tanner
	Local school
	Provincial college
1843	Ecole Normale
	Study of and interest in crystals
1848	Discovery about crystals
1850s	Meeting with alcohol manufacturer
	Interest in fermentation
	Experiments – finding of ferments
1895	Death

Louis Pasteur

In 1822 Louis Pasteur was born in the east of France, near Switzerland. His father had been a sergeant-major in Napoleon's army, but at the time of Louis' birth, he was a tanner, a man who turned the skin of an animal into leather. Louis, having shown special skill in art and science at the local school, went to the Royal College at the provincial centre at Besançon. In 1843 he entered the Ecole Normale in Paris. While he was studying there, he became interested in crystals, the form taken by certain substances when they change from a liquid into a solid. A few years later, in 1848, he made an important discovery about the properties of crystals in relation to light.

From the mid-1850s on, after being approached by an alcohol manufacturer, he became interested in fermentation. On experimenting with sour or fermented milk, he found very small bodies, the ferments, with the help of a microscope. This discovery led to Pasteur's famous work on germs or microbes. For many centuries people had believed in 'spontaneous generation', i.e. that life could start from nothing. In his work on fermentation in wine and beer, Pasteur, however, was able to show that life was always present in the form of germs, but that the number of germs in the air varied in different places and under different conditions.

Following on from this work on fermentation, Pasteur began to study other infections and diseases. He demonstrated the importance of a sterile environment, obtained through cleanliness and heat. Before his death in 1895, he had made many important contributions to science and his discoveries had saved the lives of many people. In English and other languages, his name was given to the process of heating milk in order to kill the disease-carrying bacteria: pasteurisation.

12 Big Ben

Read the following passage through quickly and look at the exercises. Then read the passage through slowly. Remember to use the context to help you guess the meanings of unfamiliar words. You won't need to understand the exact meaning of all the words in order to do the exercise.

Big Ben is one of the most famous clocks in the world. Strictly speaking the name does not refer to the whole clock but only to the bell that tolls the hours. The original bell was cast on 6th August 1856 at Norton near Stockton-on-Tees. A pair of furnaces each able to take ten tons of metal had been prepared the month before and pouring in the metal took over an hour. At the beginning of the following year the 16-ton bell was hung in New Palace Yard in London where it was rung for fifteen minutes each week to test its tone.

It had a varied journey from Norton to London and first went to West Hartlepool by rail. There it was loaded on to a ship which it badly damaged by dropping too suddenly on to the deck. When it arrived in the Port of London it was pulled across Westminster Bridge on a truck drawn by sixteen white horses.

During its development Big Ben was to suffer two cracks. It was placed in the Clock Tower in 1859 and its first day of service as a timekeeper was probably 31st of May of that year. In September the bell cracked and remained silent for three years during which time there was much argument about the cause of the crack. The solution was to give the bell a quarter turn so that it offered a different striking surface to the hammer and the weight of the hammer was reduced. This was a much less drastic solution than that following the four-foot-long crack that had appeared towards the end of its year in New Palace Yard. Following this crack the bell was melted down and reproduced in a slightly smaller form in February 1858. It was now nine feet in diameter and three tons lighter. In May of the following year it was hauled up into the clock tower in Westminster and suspended on enormous iron girders.

a   Ten of the following sentences are about the ten stages in the development of Big Ben. Put them in the correct order to outline Big Ben's history. To do this write one of the letters A–L in the first column in the table.

A   It was hung in the clock tower.
B   The 10 ton bell was hung on great girders.
C   It was turned and brought into service again.
D   The bell cracked.
E   A bell weighing 16 tons was taken to London.
F   The bell was damaged on its sea voyage.
G   A crack appeared.
H   It was rung as part of the clock.
I   Special furnaces were prepared.
J   The 13-ton bell went to Westminster.
K   As a result it was made smaller.
L   It was rung outside the clock.

Stages of Development	Letter	Year
1		
2		
3		
4		
5		
6		
7		
8		
9		
10		

b   In the second column in the table above write the year in which each event took place.

13

13 Christopher Wren

Here is a list of dates in the life of one of Britain's most famous architects – Christopher Wren. Read it through and mark where you think each paragraph should begin and end. You will probably need three or four paragraphs. After doing this, write an account of the life of Christopher Wren, using the connections suggested earlier. You need not include all the information.

Christopher Wren

1582	Galileo, in Italy, put forward his Laws of Motion
	beginning of the Age of New Learning
1632	Birth of C.W.
	interest in astronomy
1647	making of a weather-clock
	interest in anatomy
1649	at university in Oxford
1653	Master of Arts Degree
	study and research in astronomy and physics
1657	appointment as Professor of Astronomy in London
1660	co-founder of the Royal Society, for research in science
1663	design of first building – the Sheldonian Theatre in Oxford
1665	visit to Paris. Great Plague in London – many deaths
1666	C.W.'s return to London. Great Fire of London – many buildings, including St. Paul's Cathedral, burned to the ground.
	C.W.'s plan of a new design for the City of London.
1670	C.W. appointed Chief Architect
1670–1	design of twenty churches
1673	designed model for a new St. Paul's
1675	commencement of work on new St. Paul's
1711	completion of St. Paul's
1723	Death of C.W.

14 The Port of Wye

The simplest definition of a port is a place where it is possible to transfer goods between waterborne transport and land transport. The port of Wye has developed into a major British port over a period of nearly 2000 years.

Use the information in the diagrams below to help you *outline* the stages in the development of the Port of Wye.

Write between one and two pages.

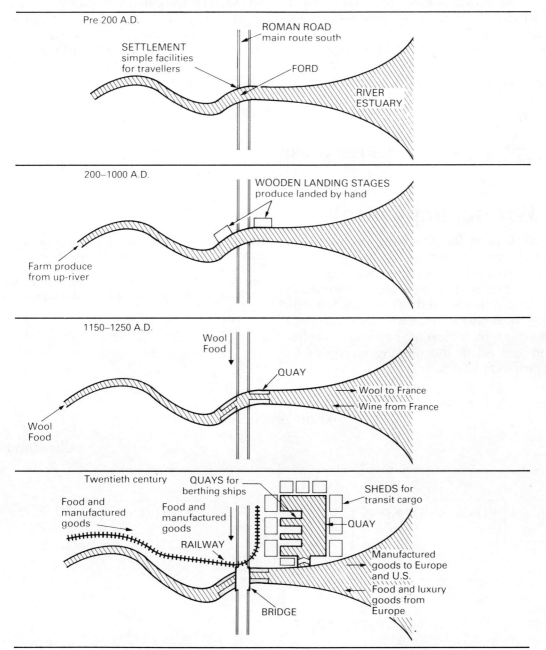

Pre 200 A.D.

ROMAN ROAD
main route south

SETTLEMENT
simple facilities
for travellers

FORD

RIVER ESTUARY

200–1000 A.D.

WOODEN LANDING STAGES
produce landed by hand

Farm produce
from up-river

1150–1250 A.D.

Wool
Food

QUAY

Wool to France

Wine from France

Wool
Food

Twentieth century

QUAYS for
berthing ships

SHEDS for
transit cargo

Food and
manufactured
goods

Food and
manufactured
goods

QUAY

RAILWAY

Manufactured
goods to Europe
and U.S.

Food and luxury
goods from
Europe

BRIDGE

'FORD'. A place for crossing the river on foot

15

Classification

1 Word lists

When we divide things into groups, we are classifying them or using a process of classification, e.g.

chairs   apples   rice   tables   eggs

apples
rice   can be classified as FOOD
eggs

chairs
tables   can be classified as FURNITURE

So FOOD is the general or group word, and apples, rice and eggs are examples or specific words. Apples could be a group word if we were interested in different types of apples, e.g. green / red, sweet / sour, cooking / eating.

2 Writing implements

If we look at the following list of words: pencil, fountain pen, chalk, ball-point pen, felt-tipped pen, typewriter, we could classify them as writing implements. By examining the similarities and differences, we could sub-divide them. In the following classification diagram, look at the bases for classification and fill in the missing words in the appropriate boxes.

Writing implements can be divided into two groups, according to whether they are machines or not. Typewriters fall into the category of machines. Implements that are not machines can be further classified on the basis of whether or not a type of ink is used.

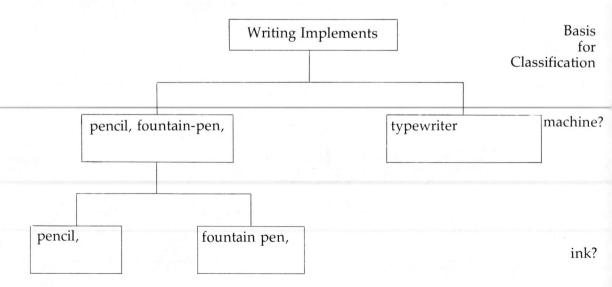

16

3 Personal communication

Telephone, letter, two-way radio, talking face-to-face, telex, smoke signal, telegram.

What do all these things have in common? They are all methods or means of personal communication. We can organise/order/ classify these examples further, but first we must find a suitable basis for classification. Possible bases may be:

Medium: speech or writing.
Chronology: listing them as they first appeared in history.

Cost: in money or effort or time.
Effectiveness: in relation to distance, speed, or length of the communication.

You can probably think of other examples and other bases.

By using a classification diagram or a list, divide and group the examples on each of the suggested bases.

e.g. *Means of Personal Communication*

Speech
talking face-to-face
telephone
two-way radio

Writing
letter
telex
telegram
smoke signal?

4 Categories 1

In the following exercise list as many examples as you can think of under two of these group headings:

Means of transport
Types of accommodation
Holidays
Sports
Heating
Advertising media
Types of government

You now have large lists of examples. To organise them, think carefully about what basis of classification will be most useful for each group. Here are some common bases and you may think of others.

Chronological
Spatial: the places where they occur
Source: where they come from or originate
Type of energy or power used
Public or Private: in use and/or ownership.
Type of equipment: the equipment or machinery used
Popularity
Effectiveness
Cost
Size

Now classify your examples, using a classification diagram or a list, depending on your basis. Keep your classifications as you will need them in a later exercise, on page 25.

17

5 Hand-held cameras

Read the following passage and then draw a classification diagram.

Hand-held cameras are of three basic types. The first of these is the direct vision camera which has a short focus lens. This camera is suitable for sports pictures and other press photography where there is limited light available. Twin-lens reflex cameras are the next category and are popular among professional photographers. Industrial and fashion photography are areas in which this camera is used. However, the world's most popular camera design is the single lens reflex camera, the uses of which vary from scientific photography, where the camera body may be attached to a microscope, to portraits, particularly of children and animals. This last type of camera is available either in an automatic or semi-automatic form. In one kind of automatic camera the aperture is set automatically, and in the other, the shutter speed is automatic.

6. Energy

a   Study the following diagram on energy.

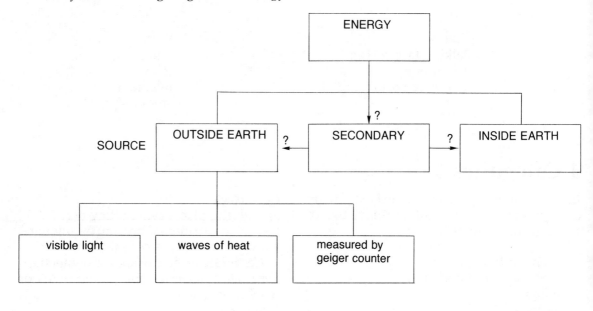

b Now read the following passage, and put one or more of the letters X, Y, O, S, M, C in the appropriate box.

The life that the earth can support depends on the amount of energy available. Organisms living on the face of the earth as it floats around in space can receive energy from several sources. Energy from outside comes to use as sunlight, and a little is reflected to us as moonlight and is brought to earth by cosmic radiation and meteors. Some of this radiation from outer space, or energy source X, can be detected and measured by telescopes while some is detected by geiger counters.

In a finer classification than would be useful for our purposes, it might be possible to divide sources detectable by telescope into two groups – those that reach the earth as waves of visible light would be Y and those that reach us as waves of heat, as from the sun for instance, would be O. Radiation measurable by geiger counter would be S.

Ignoring this possibility, however, we can now con-sider energy source M which can be said to come from the earth itself. Internally the earth is heated by radio-activity and also gains heat energy from the tidal friction that is gradually slowing down our rotation. On top of this, man is tapping enormous amounts of stored energy by burning fossil fuels like coal which, though they are buried in the earth, can be said to have come indirectly from the sun in that they were pro-duced by living processes. For this reason, they are often called secondary energy sources. We, however, prefer not to use the term secondary in this way, and we do not wish to see fossil fuels as a separate class C. Rather, we would, depending on the stand taken, include them with either source X or source M.

The term secondary is, we feel, best applied to all energy sources other than the sun in that they are infinitesimal compared to our daily sunshine which accounts for 99.9998% of our total energy income.

c From information given and using the classification outlined in the passage above complete the following.

A The classification uses ———— main classes of energy source.
B Our primary source of energy belongs to class ————.
C Fossil fuels are unlike class M if their source is seen to be ———— the earth.
D The proportion of energy released by meteors entering the earth's atmosphere could be estimated if we knew what proportion of ———— % of our total energy it repre-sented.
E A secondary energy source is one that supplies energy in ———— amounts.
F Those who believe that oil comes from a source similar to ———— will include it in class X.
G Secondary sources of energy account for ———— % of the energy total.

19

7 House types

The following passage is on house types. What do houses look like in different parts of the world? Are they all the same? What are the various types of roofs and walls? Why are there so many differences? Think about these questions, then read the passage. Remember, to do the exercise, you don't need to understand every single word; use the context to help you make intelligent guesses at meanings of unfamiliar words.

Houses vary in general appearance from area to area throughout the world. This variation occurs in response to a wide range of factors like climate, materials available and stage of technological development, and it manifests itself in differences in shape, wall thickness, roof type and the like.

Taking only three of these features – those of wall thickness, roof slope and roof extent – and examining them in terms of adaptation to climatic conditions, we find we can establish several different classes of house.

Some houses have walls which may be from one to several feet thick. Such walls may occur in hot areas where they will be constructed of brick or stone and act as insulation against heat from outside. On the other hand, such walls may consist of two thin outside layers of materials like wood or concrete with a thicker layer of some type of insulating material like fibreglass in between. This has the effect of keeping heat in. Though the two walls described above have developed in response to opposite types of climate we will call them both type 1, as they contrast sharply with houses which are quite open at the sides or are fitted with 'curtain' type walls made of thin, light material that can be rolled up to allow maximum ventilation in hot areas. In such cases the roof is supported by a series of upright poles so that the wall is not an integral part of the construction of the house. We will label the latter, wall type 2. There is of course, a range of other walls between these extremes but we will put all these together and call them type 3.

Similarly we notice a variety of roof shapes from flat to rounded to an inverted V shape. If we again take two extremes we can establish type 1 which is flat and often occurs in areas where it is pleasant to be able to utilise the relative cool of the evening air by sleeping on the roof. In contrast to this, roofs have developed with a steep slope coming from a central beam. These can be called type 2 and have the effect of throwing off snow and rain, both of which would cause roofs to sag if allowed to settle.

Some roofs are flush with the walls of the house while some extend in varying degrees beyond the line of the wall. Overhangs have developed for different purposes. Where there is a lot of snow they provide a snow-free path around the house. Where there is a lot of rain they keep the walls dry. Where there is a lot of sun they provide shade. In some cases overhangs have developed into verandas in that the edges are supported by poles. This has usually arisen in response to the need for providing a shaded place outside the house for cooking and recreation.

Together with open walls this feature provides good ventilation in hot areas. If we make our classification according to appearance (though there is a certain overlap of function) we can label the supported overhangs type 1 and the other type of overhang becomes type 2. A variation of type 1 occurs where houses are built close together. In this case a covering stretches from house to house to provide a covered pathway.

When we study the combination of these features as they occur in areas throughout the world we find we can isolate several house classes. Six possibilities are outlined in the following table.

Class	Wall Type	Roof Type	Overhang Type
I	1	1	—
II	1	1	2
III	1	2	2
IV	2	2	1
V	2	2	2
VI	3	2	2

20

a Before you read on, summarise the information in the passage by filling in the following table with notes and/or diagrams.

The first row, wall types, has been done for you.

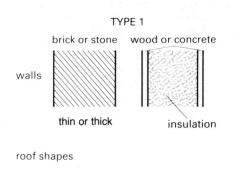

	TYPE 1	TYPE 2	TYPE 3
walls	brick or stone — thin or thick; wood or concrete — insulation	'curtain' roll up	between 1 & 2
roof shapes			
overhang			

b Here are some house descriptions. Classify the houses described as to wall type, roof type and overhang type according to the table on the opposite page. Where appropriate write I, II, III, IV, V or VI in the space provided. Write X if the house belongs to a class not discussed.

(i) A typical house of the area by the river utilises reeds in its construction. They provide the thin light walls which can be rolled up to allow the slightest breeze to penetrate. Reeds are also used to thatch the steeply sloping roofs in such a way that there is maximum protection against the heavy seasonal rains. The poles supporting the verandas on four sides come from a near-by forest as does the central roof beam running the length of the house.
Class . . . . .

(ii) This house is built of white stone which shimmers in the hot sun of the middle of the day. The walls are thick and the windows and doors very small to ensure maximum protection from the heat. The flat roof of the same area as the floor space and meeting the walls at right angles is often used by the family as a sleeping place in the hottest months of the year.
Class . . . . .

(iii) On the side of a steep mountain, this house is almost buried in snow for several months of the year. The slate roof is built at a sharp angle from a central beam and juts out beyond the line of the walls to such an extent that, even in the severest winter a passage-way free of snow surrounds the house. The walls are several feet thick utilising timber from the coniferous forest below as a framework. Fibre-glass insulation had to be transported up the mountain by pack-horse. Further warmth comes from a central heating burner which also utilises wood from the forest.
Class . . . . .

(iv) A house thought of as typical of polar regions has walls which are very thick indeed in order to keep out the biting cold of the long winter months. They are constructed of large bricks of ice. Entrance is by way of an undergound passage-way which further protects against penetration of cold air from outside. The house has the shape of an inverted basin and for some months disappears completely under a drift of snow.
Class . . . . .

(v) Ali's house is situated in an area close to a big river which is subject to annual flooding. To combat this factor, it stands on bamboo stilts to keep it above flood level. It is in a row of houses of similar design. The walls are open to the weather but protection against the heat of the sun is provided by flat overhangs which are supported by bamboo poles attached to a wooden platform which surrounds the living area of each house. The covered walkways thus provided join each house in the row to the houses next door. A certain amount of privacy is provided by 'walls' made of light flax hangings dyed in many colours. The flat roofs are made of corrugated iron.
Class . . . . .

21

8 Dams

The sources of water today are much the same as they were thousands of years ago. We still rely mainly on rivers, lakes, springs and wells but now we exploit them more extensively. We have increased the storage of natural lakes by building dams and have created new reservoirs by using dams to impound water in river valleys. Several factors have to be considered before deciding what type of dam to build and where to build it. They must be strong enough to resist the great pressure of the water that builds up behind them to form the lake upstream of the dam.

In places where the underlying rock can withstand an enormous weight, an A class dam can be constructed. Such dams are made of concrete or masonry. Built in a straight line across a water course they resist pressure by weight alone.

In the few sites where there is a narrow gorge with strong walls, a curved concrete wall can be built across the river so that the force of the water is transferred to the cliff sides. This B class dam relies on its shape for its stability rather than its weight. It contains much less concrete than an A class dam and is cheaper to construct. A B class dam is much thinner than an A class dam and has basically perpendicular sides spreading a little at the base. In the case of an A class dam, however, though the profile of the upstream face is similar to the B class dam, the downstream face is built with a steep slope.

Sometimes, as in the case of the Hoover Dam in the United States, an AB class dam is constructed. As its label implies, it combines features of the A and B class dams and uses both the shape of an arch and weight for stability. It appears as a curved version of an A class dam.

In a wide valley, what is basically a modification of a B class dam may be built. It usually consists of a series of short arches supported by buttresses jutting out into the water on the downstream side. The arches slope at an angle of about 45° on the upstream face so that water bears down on the dam and helps to give it stability. Sometimes flat slabs of reinforced concrete are used instead of arches. This latter type represents a BX class dam and the multiple arch type is BY.

a   Make a summary of the information in the passage by writing brief notes in the following table.

	material used	shape	profile	thickness
A				
B				
AB				
BX				
BY				

22

b Classify the dams shown in the following diagrams. Write one of the symbols A, B, AB, BX, BY in the box in the top right-hand corner of each diagram. If the dam is of a type not described in the passage write X. Notice that the arrows on the diagram indicate the direction of the water flow.

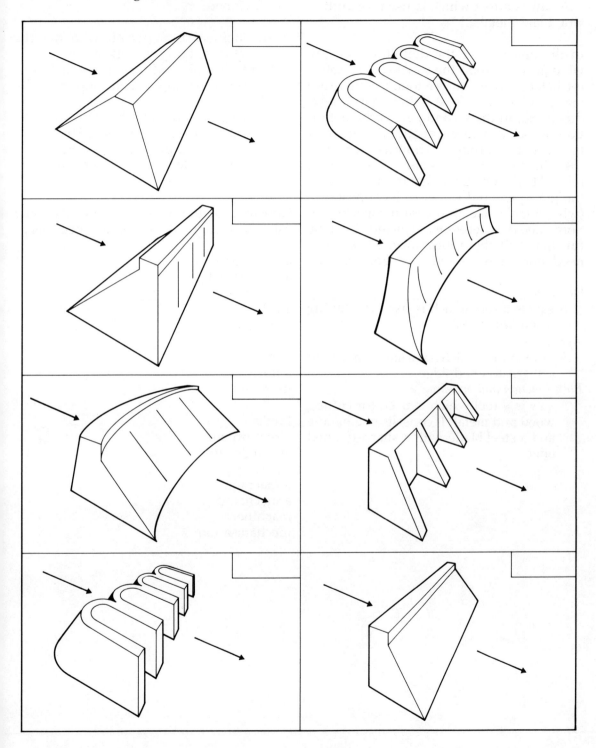

23

9 Definitions

Definitions are a form of classification, e.g.

A saw is a tool which is used for cutting wood and metal.

In the first part of the definition, we say what general group the word we are defining belongs to: A saw is a tool. But there are many different tools, e.g. hammer, screwdriver. So, in the second part of the definition, we say something about this particular member of the group and how it differs from the other members. This difference could be related to its function (what it is used for, or the job a person does) or to its appearance (what it looks like and what it consists of). Sometimes it is necessary to include both the function and the appearance, so we may need more than one sentence. For example:

Function
A saw is a tool which is used for cutting wood and metal.
Appearance
A saw is a tool which has a steel blade with a sharp-toothed edge.
Both function and appearance
A saw is a tool which is used for cutting wood and metal. It consists of a handle and a steel blade with a sharp-toothed edge.

Look at the next examples and decide whether the function or appearance or both are described.

An engineer is a person who designs machines, bridges, railways etc.
A table is a piece of furniture which consists of a flat top, usually supported by three or four legs.
Gravity is a force which attracts objects towards the centre of the earth.
A secretary is a person who works in an office and deals with letters, records, appointments etc.

Now write definitions of the following. Only use a dictionary if it is absolutely necessary.

a telephone
a telephonist

a tribe
tribalisation

water
a hose
irrigation

English
Great Britain
an Englishman

a machine
a mechanic
machinery
mechanisation

24

10 Television; the geography of Britain

The sentences in the following paragraphs are not in their correct order. Rewrite the sentences putting them into their proper order. Remember the more general statement usually comes first.

Television

A. In the second group, the companies that run the television stations receive their money from advertising.
B. Television networks can be broadly classified into two types, on the basis of how they are financed.
C. This type is known as non-commercial television.
D. Such an organisation, which therefore shows advertisements or commercials, is called commercial television.
E. In the first group the money is provided by the government.

The Geography of Britain

A. The highland area comprises the whole of Scotland, Wales, Devon and Cornwall in the south-west of England, and parts of the north-west of England.
B. The other region, the lowlands, lies mainly in the south-east of England.
C. This highland area, however, is not continuous but also contains valleys and plains.
D. Geographically, the island of Great Britain can be roughly divided into two main regions, highlands and lowlands.
E. The area contains all the mountainous parts of Great Britain and extensive uplands lying above 300 metres.

11 Categories 2

Using the useful words below, write two or three paragraphs, based on the examples you classified earlier, under two of the seven headings on page 17, exercise 4.

to divide	class	according to(whether)
to classify	group	on the basis of
to put into	category	depending on.
to fall in	type	
to group	kind	
	sort	
	part	

Comparison and Contrast

1 Colour television sets

Look at the table below and read the questions and answers which follow it.

Colour Television Sets

Model	Price £	Country of Origin	Tube Size cm	Dimensions (height × width × depth) cm	Weight kg
A	323	Japan	47	45 × 65 × 51	30
B	299	Japan	45	45 × 63 × 38	30
C	385	West Germany	45	38 × 57 × 38	23
D	324	United Kingdom	45	40 × 58 × 38	26

a   Similarities

How is Model A similar *to* Model B?

               is *the same* weight *as* Model B.

Model A   weighs *the same as* Model B.

               is *as* heavy *as* Model B.

In what ways are Models A and B similar?
    Models A and B are *similar in that* they were both made in the same country.

What are the similarities between Models A and B?
    Model A is *similar to* Model B *in* height.

What do Model A and Model B have *in common*?
    They have a 45cm height *in common*.

How does Model A *resemble* Model B?
    Model A *resembles* Model B *in* height and weight.

Now write similar questions and answers about the other models.

26

b Differences

How is Model B *different from* Model A?
   B costs *less than* A.
   B is *less* expensive *than* A.
   B is *different from* A *in* price.
   B costs £299 *while* A costs £323.

How does Model A *differ from* Model B?
   Model A *differs from* B *in* depth.
   Model A is dee*per than* B.
   Model A has a grea*ter* depth *than* B.
   Model A is 51 cm deep *whereas* B is only 38 cm deep.

What are the differences between Models A and B?
   Model A is more expensive than B, has a larger tube size, and is wider and deeper
   than B.
   As regards size,
   With regard to size,
   As far as size *is concerned,*   Model A is generally larger than Model B.
   With respect to size,
   Regarding size,
   Model A costs £323, *in contrast to* Model B, which costs £299.

Now give similar questions and answers about the differences between the other
models.

c Comparing more than two things

Which television set would you advise a friend to buy?
   If the main concern was weight, I'd advise a friend to buy Model C
   because it's *the* ligh*test* of the three.
            it weighs *the least.*

If you're uncertain?
   On the one hand Model B is the cheapest, *but on the other hand* Model C is the lightest.

Write similar sentences where the main concern is (i) price, (ii) tube size, (iii) general
dimensions.

2 Binoculars

a Read the passage and then using the information in it, fill in the gaps in the table following.

Three-pairs of binoculars, models A, B and C, will be compared with respect to the following factors: price, weight and the width of the field of view at a distance of 1,000 metres. Model A, which costs £15.75, is by far the cheapest of the three, Models B and C costing £48 and £131 respectively. Model A is as heavy as model B, weighing 1050 grams, whereas model C, the lightest, weighs only 750 grams. Regarding the user's field of view when focusing at 1000 metres, Models A and C are similar – the field of view of model C, at 102 metres, being 6 metres wider than that of Model A.

Make	Country of Origin	Price £	Weight g.	Field of view at 1000 m. m.	Shortest Focusing Distance m.	Free from Optical Defects	Contrast	Quality of Construction	Handling
A	Korea				12	****	****	***	***
B	Japan			145	6	***	****	**	***
C	West Germany				5	**	****	***	*****
D	Hong Kong	24.00	900	90	7	***	***	**	**
E	German Democratic Republic	75.00	1050	130	4	***	****	****	****

* The more asterisks, the better

b You have been asked to recommend a pair of binoculars. Write a paragraph explaining why you recommend one model rather than the others.

3 Concession and addition: connectives

a When we want to show that something is different from what we would normally expect, we signal this by using a linking word of contrast.

X It was the most expensive model. Y He bought it.

X *but* Y It was the most expensive model *but* he bought it.
Although X, Y.
Despite
In spite of its be*ing* the most expensive model, Y.
Despite the cost of the model, Y.
X *yet* Y.
X. *However*, Y.
X. *Nevertheless*, Y.
X. *Notwithstanding this*, Y.

28

b   To draw attention to the combination of two similar things, or aspects of the same thing, the following expressions can be used:

It was the smallest model *and* the lightest.
It was the smallest *and also* the lightest model.
It was the smallest model, *and* cost the least *as well*.
It was *not only* the smallest model, *but* it cost the least *as well*.
It was the smallest model. *In addition,* it cost the least.
Furthermore,
In addition to being the smallest model, it cost the least.
It was the smallest model *as well as* being the cheapest.

4 Personal transport

a   Read the following passage and underline the linking devices for comparison and contrast.

Subject: Compare and contrast two methods of personal transport.

Cars and bicycles are similar in that they are both privately owned means of transport. In other words, they have in common the fact that the owner can decide when and where to go. However, there are a lot of differences between them. A car costs a lot more to buy than a bicycle. In addition, it is far more expensive to run. For example, a car has to be insured, and must be serviced regularly; furthermore, spare parts for a car cost a lot of money. A car uses petrol, which is expensive, whereas a bicycle uses only human energy. On the other hand, as far as comfort is concerned, a car is better than a bicycle. In a car you are protected from the weather, have comfortable seats and plenty of room to carry people and luggage. A car is not only more comfortable than a bicycle, but it is faster as well. With respect to convenience, it is difficult to say which one is better. A bicycle is certainly easier to park! To sum up, each one has its advantages and disadvantages.

Analysis:

Factors to consider	Car	Bicycle
Purchase cost	£2,000	£50
Running cost per year	£500	£5
Speed	+	−
Comfort	+	−
Convenience	?	?

b   Now draw up a similar chart comparing two other means of transport, and then write a passage based on the chart.

5 Tables and charts: useful expressions

As you have seen, tables and charts are useful in presenting information of comparison and contrast. Here are some of the expressions we use with these and other statistical forms.

According to the statistics,
table,
graph,
figures presented,

We can see
It can be seen
from the statistics that

As is shown
As can be seen
in the table

6 University students

a Study the chart below and then read the sentences on the opposite page which show the different ways we use to describe numbers and percentages.

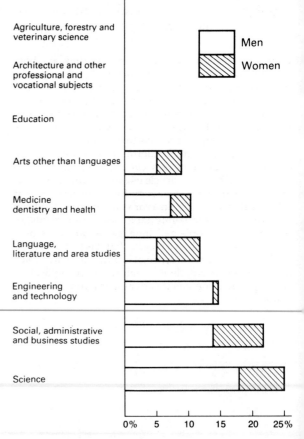

University full-time students: subject groups of study United Kingdom

30

A *greater number* of men studied science than engineering.

A *larger proportion* of women studied social, administrative and business studies than engineering.

Science accounted for *the largest percentage* of male students.

There was nearly *double the number* of women studying languages, compared with the number studying medicine.

There were about *twice as many* men studying engineering as those studying medicine.

The number of men studying science was over *three times as large* as that studying languages.

b   Fill in the chart for the first three areas according to the following information.

According to the chart, the total number of students doing arts was nearly as great as that doing medicine, making up about 9% of the total. In arts, there were equal numbers of men and women. In education also, men made up fifty per cent of the students, who totalled about 4% of all university students. However, in architecture, there were three times as many men as women, together making a total of 3% of all students. Finally, the situation for agriculture was the same as for architecture.

c   Fill in the gaps in the following sentences from the chart. Each group of dots represents one word.

(i)   A . . . . . number of female students studied language and literature . . . . . male students.

(ii) In other arts subjects, there were slightly . . . . . men . . . . . women.

(iii) There were about . . . . male students as female ones in medicine, dentistry and health.

(iv) Women made up only a very . . . . of engineering students, about . . . . . % of the total.

Now write similar sentences comparing the numbers of men and women in social, administrative and business studies, and in science.

31

7 Education systems

The following table gives information about the education systems of three different countries. Using this information compare and contrast the education system of countries A, B and C. Remember, do not try to include every detail but just say what is similar and what is different. An introductory paragraph has been written for you.

A study of education systems throughout the world reveals certain basic similarities from country to country. It also shows, however, differing attitudes to a wide range of factors. These include things like school leaving age, length and type of compulsory education, age of specialisation, and so on. Probably the simplest way of illustrating the pattern of similarities and differences is to look at the situation in two or three selected countries. For instance, we can compare the education systems of countries A B and C.

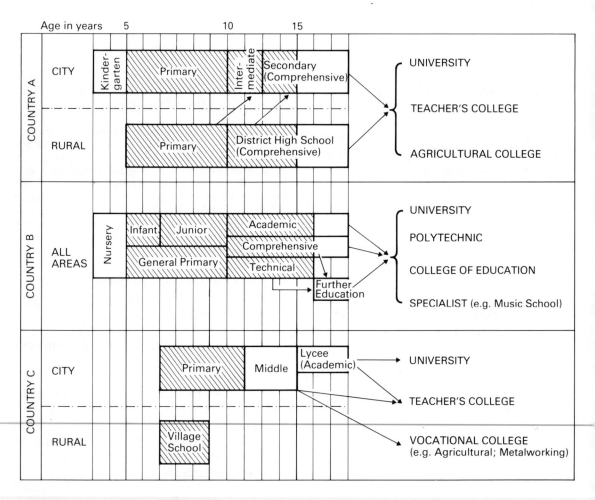

Compulsory Education

8 Increase and decrease: useful expressions

Here is a list of expressions used in describing the sort of chart which shows increase or decrease.

rapid
sharp
steep
dramatic
marked

slow
slight
gradual
barely noticeable

a rise
an increase
to increase
to shoot up

a fall
a decrease
a reduction
to decline
to reduce

9 Water shortage

Read the following passage and then, using the information contained in it, complete the graph that follows it.

The present shortage of water in a growing number of communities in the U.S. is the result primarily of increased consumption of water rather than of any important change in the natural supply. Not only has our population increased but our per capita use of water has risen – and at a much greater rate. In Texas, for instance, while the population increased by three hundred per cent in the fifty-year period ending in 1940, the use of water for industrial and municipal purposes increased about thirty times; for irrigation about fifty-five times and for water power about eighty-five times; for all purposes the average overall increase was almost seventy-one times. Similar increases in the use of water have occurred throughout the nation.

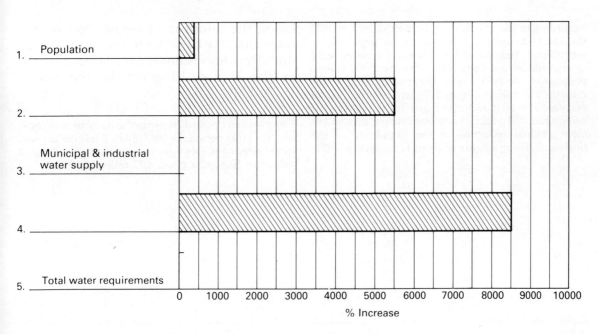

1. _____ Population

2. _____

3. _____ Municipal & industrial water supply

4. _____

5. _____ Total water requirements

0   1000   2000   3000   4000   5000   6000   7000   8000   9000   10000

% Increase

33

10 Cinema and television

Look at the following graph and read the passage.

The changes in the popularity of cinema and television 1957–1974.

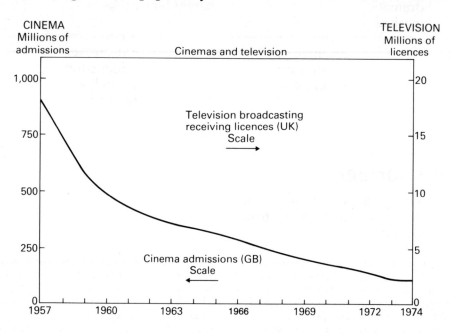

According to the graph, over the period 1957 to 1974 the trend was towards a decrease in the popularity of the cinema. There was a dramatic fall in the number of cinema admissions from 1957, when about 900 million people went, to 1959, when the attendance figure was roughly 550 million. From 1959 to 1963 the rate of decrease slowed down, the figure for the latter year being about 350 million. From this year on, there was a more gradual reduction in the popularity of the cinema, reaching a figure of about 125 million in 1974.

Using the information below, plot on the same chart the curve for the variations in the number of television viewing licences issued in the United Kingdom in the period 1957–1974.

There was an upwards trend in the number of licences issued in this period. In 1957 about 7 million licences were issued, and this figure rose steadily, reaching 14 million in 1966, to a peak of 17 million in 1974.

11 Energy consumption

a   Look at the table below and from it, fill in the gaps in the two following passages. Some gaps require more than one word.

(i) One Year – 1974
The total energy consumption in 1974 totalled just under . . . . . million tons. Petroleum made up the largest . . . . . of this figure. There was nearly as . . . . . coal used as petroleum. The amount of natural gas consumed was . . . . . of that of petroleum. Nuclear and hydroelectricity only made up a small . . . . . of the total, about 10 million tons.

(ii) Two Years – 1946 and 1962
In 1946 the total energy consumption was a little over . . . . . million tons, whereas in 1962 it rose to reach . . . . . million tons. The quantity of coal used remained . . . . . . There was an increase in the consumption of petroleum. In 1946 it was about one-tenth of that of coal, while in 1962 it was about . . . . . of that of coal.

b   Now write a passage, based on the table, describing the main trends in energy consumption over the period 1932 to 1974.

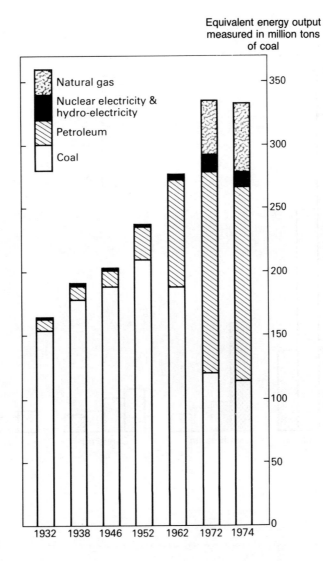

Equivalent energy output measured in million tons of coal

Natural gas

Nuclear electricity & hydro-electricity

Petroleum

Coal

35

12 Outdoor activities

Use the information in the graph to write four paragraphs about outdoor activities:

(i) Compare and contrast the relative popularity of skiing in Switzerland, France, Britain and Belgium. If possible, account for any differences.

(ii) Compare and contrast the general pattern of skiing and climbing for the four countries. If possible, account for any similarities.

(iii) Compare and contrast the relative importance of skiing, climbing, canoeing and caving in Britain. Compare this pattern with that of France.

(iv) Compare and contrast the pattern of outdoor activities as exemplified in this graph with any other country.

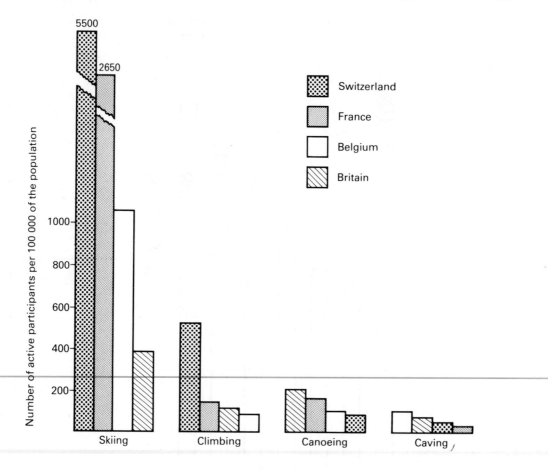

Comparative Popularity of Selected Outdoor Activities in some Western European Countries in 1968

13 Analogies

a   When we are trying to explain something that is new or a bit difficult, we often draw an analogy – that is to say, we compare it or find the similarities between it and something that is more familiar. For example, a teacher might explain the action of the heart by saying it is like a pump.

A pump is a machine for forcing liquid or gases out of something, e.g. a water pump. The heart takes blood from the veins and forces it into the arteries, i.e. it pumps blood. There are obviously many differences between a pump and a heart, but in their *action* they are similar.

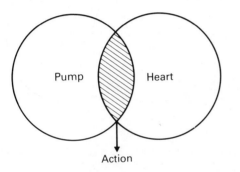

b   When we draw an analogy between two things, we have to say how they are similar. If, for instance, we say that the flow of electricity and the flow of water are similar, this is not much help; we have to say in what ways they are similar.

The flow of electricity through wires and cables from the mains supply can be compared with the flow of water through pipes from a water tank. When the tap is turned off, the water does not move, but when a tap is turned on, the height of the water in the tank exerts pressure on the water in the pipes and forces it through the outlet, i.e. the tap. This water pressure is comparable with voltage in electricity. The rate of the water flow, similar to the flow of current, is controlled by two things: the pressure and the size of the outlet. For example, a very narrow spray allows less water to flow than a wide pipe. Similarly in electricity, a very thin wire restricts or resists the flow of current. Electricians measure this resistance in ohms and the flow of the current in ampères (amps).

From the passage above, fill in the chart below.

Water	Electrical term
Pressure of water (related to height of water tank)	
Width of pipe	
Flow of water	

c   Look at the following analogies and then fill in the diagrams to show exactly what the two things compared have in common. The first one has been done for you.

(i) In the same way as bats use sound echoes, ships' navigators explore underwater with ultrasonic waves.

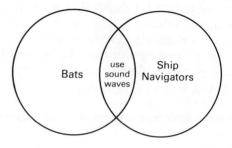

Bats | use sound waves | Ship Navigators

(ii) The part of the Earth we know best, the land and the sea, is only a thin crust covering the earth like the skin of a very slightly wrinkled apple.

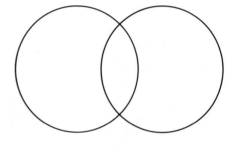

(iii) Every plant and animal is a living machine; so is every living cell. As with any other machine, a living cell needs fuel to supply it with energy.

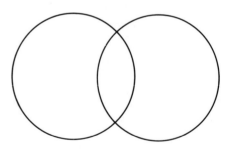

(iv) The screw attachment on a camera lens is a mechanical analogue to the small muscle in the human eye, whereby the focal length is shortened.

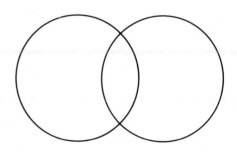

d   Read the following passage, and then fill in the chart below it.

A computer is a tool and although a very complex one, it operates on the same principles as any other tool. In other words, it takes raw material and converts it into a product by means of a device which performs a process. The workings of a computer can be illustrated with examples from banking. The raw material in this case might be a sum of money written on a cheque, that is to say, one isolated fact. The product is information, i.e. the one fact related to other facts. In the example, this might be the total withdrawals or deposits of one customer. The device is the computer itself. This is primarily a calculating machine but it can also store up a vast mass of information.

Tool	Computer	Example
raw material		
	computer	——
		total withdrawals or deposits

e   Now think about what the following have in common. For each pair draw a diagram or make a list to show the common feature(s).

the human brain and a computer

an eye and a camera

f   Sometimes two things are compared indirectly. Look at the following example.

The garden was covered in a *blanket* of snow.

What two things are being compared?
The snow in the garden is compared to a blanket.
How are they similar?
As a blanket completely covers a bed, so the snow completely covered the garden.

Now answer the two questions about the following sentences.

(i)   A traffic engineer's work is to keep the traffic *flowing*.
(ii) The teacher *herded* the children across the road.
(iii) People *flocked* to the exhibition.
(iv) The *tide* of public opinion turned against him.
(v)   Poisonous insecticides project a menacing *shadow* into the future, the shadow of sterility.
(vi) Coal consumption reached a *peak* in 1952.
(vii) Oil prices have *rocketed* in the last few years.
(viii) In compiling the dictionary, accuracy was *sacrificed* for speed.
(ix) The lecturer was *bombarded* with questions.
(x)   The earth's vegetation is part of the *web* of life, in which there are close relations between plants, animals and the earth.
(xi) The company's *target* for that year was to make £300,000 profit.
(xii) Death is but a long sleep.

Cause and Effect

1 Consequence: connectives

A common connection between ideas is that of cause and effect. If we ask why something happens, the answer is the cause. If we ask what the result of something is, then the answer is the effect. There are many different signals of this link between ideas.

a C (cause) Wealth is unevenly distributed in the world.
   E (effect) Many people die of starvation.

   E *because* C.
   Since
   As   C,   E.

   Owing to wealth being unevenly distributed in the world,   E.
               the uneven distribution of wealth in the world,
   E, *owing to the fact that* wealth is unevenly distributed.

   The fact that E is *due to* wealth being unevenly distributed.
                                the uneven distribution of wealth.
   The reason for many people dying of starvation is that C.

b C (cause) People earned more money during the 60's.
   E (effect) There was an increased percentage of home ownership.

   One effect of
   One result of   people earning more money during the 60's was *that* E.
   One consequence of
   People earning more money during the 60's *resulted in* an increased percentage of home ownership.

                                                        one effect of
   An increased percentage of home ownership was *one result of*   people
                                                        one consequence of
   earning more money during the 60's.

c C (cause) A piece of iron was left in the rain.   E (effect) It became rusty.

      C. *Therefore,* E.   C, *as a result of which,* E.
          So, E.   *as a consequence of which,* E.
          Thus, E.
          Hence, E.
          Consequently, E.
          As a consequence, E.
          As a result, E.

40

d C (cause)   The sailors' diet was deficient in Vitamin C.
   E (effect)   They suffered from scurvy.

C, *with the result that* E.
   so that

The sailors' diet was *so* deficient in Vitamin C *that* E.

There was *such* a deficiency of Vitamin C in the sailors' diet *that* E.

2 Erosion

Erosion is the wearing away of the land by various natural agencies.

	Agent	*Effect*
a.	sun	rocks expand, crack and break up.
b.	wind	carries loose particles away; with sand, helps to wear away rocks.
c.	rain	loosens and carries away soil.
d.	frost	freezes water in the cracks of rocks, cracks widen and rock breaks.
e.	rivers	wear away land, especially where the slope is steep.
f.	glaciers	wear away land.
g.	sea	wears away rocks.

Using the cause and effect links suggested, describe why erosion occurs from the information given above. The first one has been done for you.

a. causes   as a result

The heat of the sun causes the rocks to expand. As a result of this, the rocks crack and break up.

b. hence

c. the effect

d. causes   consequently

e. ?

f. ?

g. ?

41

3 Degrees of certainty

When discussing cause and effect, we often want to show how sure we are about the relationship, i.e. the degree of certainty. The following chart is a rough guide as to how we express this.

Percentage	Frequency	Certainty	Verb
100%	always	certainly undoubtedly	will must simple present tense
	usually generally as a rule		should ought to
	often	probably likely presumably	
	sometimes occasionally	possibly perhaps	can could may might
	rarely, seldom hardly ever	unlikely	
0%	never		will not cannot could not simple present tense (negative)

Below are some examples showing possibility about cause and effect in a past event.

The erosion was possibly caused by the wind.
It is possible that the erosion was caused by the wind.
The erosion may have been caused by the wind.
The erosion could have been caused by the wind.

Now, using words from the table above, do this exercise about a cure for the common cold.

These tablets cure the common cold.

Example: 0%   These tablets *cannot* cure the common cold.

Write sentences showing a degree of certainty of roughly:
(i) 15% (ii) 40% (iii) 50% (iv) 80% (v) 100%

42

4 Plants

You are a plant doctor. Read the following passage. Below it are some descriptions of unhealthy leaves. For each, write what you think may be the cause, and where possible, give directions on how to correct the condition.

There are a variety of factors to be taken into consideration when analysing why some plants become sickly or die. Dryness in the soil causes the leaves to lose freshness, or wilt, and may result in death of the plant. On the other hand, too much water may result in the leaves losing their strength and drooping, or in their becoming yellow, and occasionally in the rotting of the leaves and stems. While sunshine is necessary for plants, if it is too strong, the soil may be baked and the roots killed. However, if there is no light, the leaves will become pale and the stems thin, and if not corrected, the consequence will be the death of the plant.

(i) The leaves are yellow and several of them have fallen off.
(ii) The leaves have brown spots on them.
(iii) The leaves have wilted.
(iv) The stems and the leaves have rotted.
(v) The leaves are small and pale, and the stems are thin.

Car Problems

Many things can go wrong with a car. Here is a list of problems and their possible causes. Write sentences about the problems as in the example.

Problem	Causes
starter will not turn engine	flat battery
	or
	loose or corroded battery terminals
	or
	a jammed starter
a smell of burning	a short circuit in the wires
	or
	oil or a rag on the exhaust pipe
brakes pull to one side	a soft tyre on one side
	or
	worn linings on the brake
engine turns over but does not start	damp in the ignition system
	or
	loose leads
	or
	fuel shortage

Example:
If the starter will not turn the engine, the battery may be flat. This problem could also be caused by loose or corroded battery terminals. Alternatively, it is possibly due to a jammed starter.

5 Chinampa farming

Read the following passage

The Aztec Empire arose in the Valley of Mexico and it was based on a sophisticated system of large-scale land reclamation through drainage. The island capital of the Aztecs consisted of some 400 houses surrounded by six or eight long narrow strips of land surrounded on at least three sides by water. These gardens are called chinampas.

The chinampa zone is to the south of the valley. The rest of the valley, although it produced crops, was far less favourable to farming because of the arid climate. The chinampas however presented two major, conflicting difficulties apart from those involved in their cultivation and day to day maintenance. One of these was to keep the water level high and the other was the prevention of floods.

The valley had no external outlet for water. Year after year over the millenniums, nitrous salts had been swept down into the chinampa area by the summer rains and had been concentrated by evaporation in the eastern part of the area. It was essential to keep the deadly salts away from the chinampas. For this reason the chinampas could only function properly if they were fed constantly by freshwater springs which maintained the water level, washed off the salt and in certain areas held the salt water back. Originally there were adequate springs but the rapid growth of the Aztec capital and its associated gardens soon outstripped the available springs. The problem was solved by the construction of aqueducts to bring fresh water from mainland springs. It has sometimes been assumed that the sole purpose of the aqueducts was to carry drinking water to the island inhabitants but, if so, their thirst must have been incredible.

These aqueducts, or raised water courses, were structures of great strength and ingenuity.

The second major problem – periodic flooding by salty water – was also finally solved by construction works. The salts which had already made the eastern part of the zone unsuitable for chinampa development rose and flooded over the gardens during the summer period. According to the pollen chronology worked out for the area at Yale University, the problem became acute because the climate of the region seems to have been wetter than at any time since the end of the last Ice Age.

In the fifteenth century an enormous dike of stones held together with mud and branches was built. The wall on which 20,000 men laboured extended for ten miles and successfully sealed off the chinampa zone from encroaching flood water and also had the effect of leaving the chinampas in a freshwater zone.

Now choose the correct cause and solution for each of the two problems opposite. Cross out the wrong causes and solutions, as in the following example.

Example:
Mr. Jones had to find a new way to go to work because the train he used to go on did not run any more. After looking at the relative costs, he decided to drive to work. He therefore bought a car.

PROBLEM: *Mr. Jones had to go to work a new way.*

Cause	Solution		
A His usual train had been stopped.	A He wrote to his newspaper	so that	A he could go by bus.
B He had no car.	B He bought a car		B he could go by train.
C He did not like walking.	C He found a new train		C he could drive to work.
D He had no money.	D He sold his car		D he could walk to work.

44

i. PROBLEM: *The water level had to be kept high.*

Cause	Solution		
A The climate grew wetter.	A Fresh water pipes were introduced		A drinking water was brought by aqueducts.
		so that	
B The gardens were fed by fresh water springs.	B Fresh water springs were dug		B salt water was drained away.
C Evaporation caused salts to build up on the gardens.	C Raised water channels were built		C fresh water was brought from elsewhere.
D The inhabitants were thirsty.	D Water was brought in by boat		D an external outlet was made.

ii PROBLEM: *It was necessary to control floods*

Cause	Solution		
A The climate had become wetter.	A A big pile of stones was made		A fresh water was kept off the gardens.
		so that	
B The wet season was in summer.	B An enormous wall was built		B salty water flowed out.
C There was no fresh water in the area.	C Piles of tree branches were made		C salty water was held back.
D Salt water spread over the gardens in summer.	D A big ditch was dug in the mud		D fresh water could flow in.

6 How it works

When we want to explain how something works, we usually begin by defining and/or describing it and then give the explanation, showing the cause and effect relationships.

a Read the following passage on a violin.

A violin is a stringed musical instrument. The strings are supported by the bridge, which is connected to the main body of the violin. The movement of the strings can be effected either by hand or, more commonly, by means of a horsehair bow. The bow is drawn across the tight strings, thus causing them to vibrate. These vibrations are transferred via the bridge to the rest of the violin, making the whole body vibrate in sympathy with the strings. The frequency with which a string vibrates can be changed by altering its length, its tension or its mass.

Notice a common expression in explanations: *by means of*. Also note that we use a short form for the effect. Instead of saying 'The bow is drawn across the tight strings, *with the result that* they vibrate,' we can say

'. . .*thus* causing them to vibrate'.
       so

b Here is the beginning of an explanation of how refrigerators work.

When a liquid evaporates, it absorbs heat. If it is converted back into liquid form, called condensation, it gives off any heat it has absorbed. Refrigerators are cooled on this principle. A liquid, known as refrigerant, circulates round the heat-exchange of the refrigerator.

Now using the following notes, complete the explanation.

    liquid passes through the heat exchange
        evaporates
        absorbs heat from frozen food compartment
        is recondensed
        gives off absorbed heat through exhaust pipe at back of refrigerator

c Write down explanations of how the following work, and then think of some topics of your own.

a pair of scissors
a ball-point pen
a torch or flashlight
a lock (with a key)

46

7 Reference: connectives

In writing, and especially when writing explanations, we often have to refer back to an earlier word or idea. To make it clear that it is something we have mentioned before, we often use *this* or *these*, or sometimes *the*. In addition, to avoid repeating exactly the same word again and again, we use another word – either a different part of speech (e.g. if we use a verb the first time, we may change it to a noun the second time), or a word that has a similar meaning, or a more general word.

For example:

First Reference	*Later Reference*
The water evaporates.	This evaporation
It moves	This movement
It enlarges	This enlargement
There are changes	These variations
The temperature falls	This drop in temperature
The wood is cut with an axe.	This method of cutting
The numbers can be added, multiplied etc.	These mathematical operations
The product can be advertised on radio, TV etc.	These means of advertising

8 Petroleum

Read the following passage on petroleum.

In the shallow waters off the coast a few hundred million years ago, vast numbers of minute creatures and plants lived and died. Owing to the lack of oxygen, the remains of *these marine organisms* were unable to decompose. As a result of climatic changes, *these coastal areas* became buried under layers of earth, and *the organic remains* were subjected to high pressures and temperatures over periods of millions of years. *These conditions* caused the decomposition and the chemical breakdown of the fats, carbohydrates and proteins in the remains. As the conditions of decomposition varied from one region to another, petroleum found in different parts of the world varies considerably in composition. In the course of time petroleum was squeezed out of the original source rock into more porous rocks, in *some of which* it accumulated.

To what earlier words or phrases do the phrases in italics refer?

9 Elaboration: connectives

When we want to explain something complicated, we often describe it twice – once in a fairly complex way, and then more simply. We usually signal this with the following phrases:

    i.e. (that is)
    that is to say
    in other words

After we have made a general statement, we often follow it with an example, again to help our reader understand. These are some of the ways to introduce an example.

    e.g.
    for example
    for instance
    such as
    An example of this is
    An illustration of this is

    This can be exemplified
                illustrated
                shown
                demonstrated

    If one considers
           looks at

In the following four paragraphs the simplifying and explaining signals have been left out. Place an appropriate signal in the spaces.

(i) Waterlogged soil, ... soil that has too much water, is as bad for the growing of crops as lack of water is. Soil waterlogging can either be natural or man-made, ..., with too much irrigation.

(ii) In the nineteenth century Britain imported raw materials, ... cotton, copper, rubber, from overseas and exported manufactured goods . . . . . articles of clothing and machines.

(iii) In 1970 52% of the world's population worked in agriculture; . . . . . one man in two made his living from the land or was a member of a farming family.

(iv) There are many different types of family laws in the world. . . . . . in Britain marriages are monogamous, ..., a person is allowed to have only one spouse at a time. In parts of Africa and the Middle East, marriages can be polygamous, ... a man may have more than one wife at a time, or a woman may have more than one husband.

48

10 The water cycle

Look at the following diagram of the water cycle.

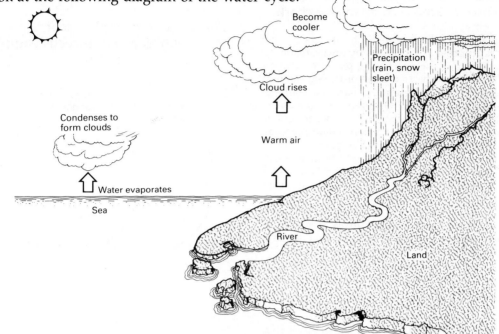

Now complete this passage describing and explaining the water-cycle.

Rain falls on the land and is carried by rivers to the sea. The heat of the sun causes the water to evaporate. The water vapour cools and condenses, thus forming clouds.

11 Vitamins

Write a paragraph on vitamins, describing them and explaining their function. Use the following notes to help you.

vitamins
1. organic substances
2. not made by the body
3. obtained from various foods
4. essential for growth and maintenance of the body
5. absence or shortage leads to various deficiency diseases

Vitamin	Food Source	Use	Deficiency Disease
e.g. A	milk, eggs, butter green vegetables liver	aids growth	night blindness
C	oranges, lemons, green vegetables, potatoes	promotes healing	scurvy
D	?	?	?

49

12 Inflation

a   Read the following passage and then fill in the spaces in the accompanying chart.

Inflation is a process of steadily rising prices, resulting in a diminishing of the purchasing power of a given nominal sum of money. In other words, you can buy fewer goods for £1 in December than you could in January of the same year. One type of inflation is known as demand-pull inflation. This occurs under conditions of full employment, when demand exceeds supply of goods; that is to say, when people want to buy more goods than are available. The process of demand-pull inflation operates as follows. An increased demand for goods leads to an increased demand for labour, resulting in higher wages and salaries. This has the effect of increasing costs of production and thus causes increased prices. However, as wages and salaries are higher, the increased demand for goods continues, and so the cycle goes on.

Demand-pull inflation

Conditions: (1) full employment
(2) demand exceeds supply at current prices.

Process:

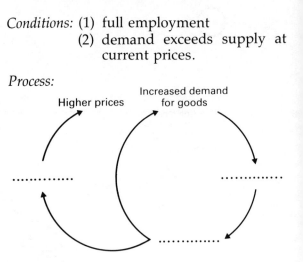

b   An example of this type of inflation is in a post-war situation. Use the notes below to explain why and how it occurs then.

Wartime conditions: Full employment – increase in numbers at work
– large overtime being worked
Consumer goods – not produced, production diverted to meet military demands

Post-war situation:
– great ability to spend, owing to savings
– strong desire to buy goods
– no goods available

50

13 Guano

a   Read the passage on guano and, as you are doing so, make notes to complete the chain of causation below.

Chain of causation: from the ocean current to the ships exporting the guano.

ocean current
↓
cold polar water, rich in nitrates, etc. off Peruvian coast
↓
warm surface water displaced with lower water, rich in essential salts
↓
· · · · ·
↓
· · · · ·
↓
· · · · ·
↓
· · · · ·
↓
fertile bird droppings; dry climate
↓
export trade

Guano

Towards the end of the last century, the republic of Peru awoke to the fact that there was to be found on certain offshore islands along their coast a source of natural wealth of the greatest value. The Peruvians could and did make use of it themselves, but what was of far greater importance for them, they found that other nations also realised its value and were anxious to buy it in enormous quantities and at a fantastic profit to the exchequer of Peru. It appeared to be inexhaustible and consisted of a compact powdery substance which was simply the droppings of seabirds, nesting there by the million, accumulated over the centuries and preserved in the rainless climate of those islands. They called it guano, and it was a fertiliser of remarkable potency, which meant so much for Peru that from the proceeds of its sale there arose public buildings in their cities, bridges over their rivers, warehouses and docks for their ports, all, so to speak, founded on birds' dung. For some years it became possible to remit taxation, so enormous was the national revenue. Two things put an end to this golden age. One was the realisation that the supply was by no means inexhaustible, that on many of the islands the spades of the excavators were scraping on the native rock. The other was the introduction of synthetic fertilisers. Today Peruvian guano is no longer important as an export, though still extensively used inside the country in the irrigated fields of the coastal desert.

The reasons for the existence of all those millions of tons of bird-droppings are strange and interesting, and investigating them reveals a long and complicated chain of causation of which one end is represented by those ships of many nations stuffing their holds with ton after ton of natural fertiliser, and the other by an ocean current. This is the great movement of water which moves northward from Antarctic waters for more than half the length of the South American continent, to a point off the coast of Peru, where it sweeps outwards in a curve into the Pacific, driven by crosswinds. Because of its polar origin the water of the current is several degrees colder than that through which it flows, and its continual displacing of the warmer surface water brings yet more cold water welling up from the depths.

All this cold water makes the northward-sweeping current particularly rich in the nitrates and phosphates on which plant life in the sea, as elsewhere, depends. Polar seas are consistently richer in these substances than waters nearer the equator. Then there is the water brought near the surface from far below, along the course of the current. Marine organisms sink, when they die, to the ocean floor and accumulate in deep drifts to form a great reservoir of these essential salts, with the result that water brought up from these deeper levels is more heavily charged with them than would otherwise be the case at that particular latitude. On this continuously renewed supply of vital elements an enormous wealth of microscopic marine plants flourishes exceedingly, providing an almost inexhaustible supply of food for the minute creatures which in their turn provide food for the vast numbers of fish. The fish similarly encourage and support, to complete the chain of cause and effect, the teeming life of the Bird Islands of Peru, one of the wonders of the world.

b   Using the notes you have made, describe why there are unusually large numbers of birds off the Peruvian coast.

51

Advantages and Disadvantages

1 Essay plan

Often when we discuss something, there are things to be said in favour of it and things to be said against it. So, before we reach a decision and express our opinion, we try to weigh up the 'fors' and 'againsts' or the 'pros' and 'cons'.

Before beginning to write then, draw up a list of the advantages and disadvantages and try to classify these into some sort of order. You'll also need to think of something to write for a general introduction and for a general conclusion. Here is a plan for an essay on the topic 'Everybody Should Retire at 50'. You are given the introduction and first part of the essay. By using the plan and ideas of your own, complete the essay.

'Everybody Should Retire at 50'

Introduction: Why is there retirement?
At what age now?

Analysis: public and personal arguments

Body of Essay:	*Advantages*	*Disadvantages*
public	more jobs faster promotion	loss of experienced people cost of pensions less tax paid
personal	time to do what one wants while still healthy	people don't know how to use leisure some people enjoy working

Conclusion: Other points: self-employed people?
compulsory/voluntary?
Decision, or reasons for no decision.

Introduction

Compulsory retirement from employment is a fairly recent phenomenon. It implies that work is not something that most people enjoy and that, after a certain number of years of working, men and women should be rewarded, set free and left to enjoy themselves for the rest of their lives. It could also have the implication that, at a certain age, one is no longer fit enough for work, and, on grounds of inefficiency, one should stop working. In most countries the present age of retirement is between 55 and 70. Now the suggestion is that this age should be brought down to 50, so that when people reach this age, they stop being employed and start receiving a state pension.

Analysis

This is a complex subject and there are many points to be said both for and against. First of all, I would like to look at this subject from the viewpoint of the state or public, and then consider the more personal arguments.

Public: advantages and disadvantages

Jobs

In a world of rising unemployment one advantage of an earlier age of retirement is that there would be more opportunites for jobs for younger people. Moreover, ambitious younger workers would be able to reach the top without a lot of older people blocking the way. However, if age is equated with experience, can a country afford to lose the services of a large number of experienced workers? In addition, the cost to the country of an earlier retirement age should be considered.

Cost

If there were more people receiving pensions, this would cost the government a lot of money. At the same time, there would be fewer people paying taxes. Consequently, the extra money for the pensions would have to come from the working younger people, which could lead to a great deal of dissatisfaction.

Now complete this essay using the plan opposite.

2 Essay titles

Here are some other suggestions for topics to write about. Remember to look at both sides, draw the comparisons and contrasts, give reasons and above all, plan and organise carefully.

All public transport should be free.

Voting for elections should be compulsory.

Capital punishment is the only effective deterrent to crime.

All men are born equal.

National boundaries should be abolished.